LAW ON FOOD SAFETY

Essential Legal Terms Explained You Need To Know About Law on Food Safety!

DR. PETER JOHNSON

Copyright © 2019

All rights reserved.

ISBN: 9781092578288

TEXT COPYRIGHT © [DR. PETER JOHNSON]

Table of Contents

Introduction

Thank you and congratulate you for downloading the book *"LAW ON FOOD SAFETY: Essential Legal Terms Explained You Need To Know About law on food safety!"*

With a clear, concise, and engaging writing style, Dr. Peter Johnson will help you with a practical understanding of food safety law topics about *principles of food safety management, state policies on food safety, prohibited acts, handling of violations of the law on food safety, rights and obligations of food traders, rights and obligations of food consumers, food advertisement, food safety inspection;* provide you a road map to navigating law on food safety rules and help you build a foundation for understanding the overall picture and **much much more**. This book delivers extensive coverage of every aspect of the law and details the duties a paralegal is expected to perform when working within law on food safety. High-level, comprehensive coverage is combined with cutting-edge developments and foundational concepts.

As the author of the book, I promise this book will be *an invaluable source of legal reference for professionals, international lawyers, law students, business professionals* and anyone else who want to improve their use of legal terminology, succinct clarification of legal terms and have a better understanding of law on lawyers. All legal terms and phrases are well written and explained clearly in plain English.

Thank you again for purchasing this book, and I hope you enjoy it.

Let's get started!

General Provisions

Law on food safety provides for rights and obligations of organizations and individuals in assuring food safety: conditions for assuring safety of foods and food production, trading, import and export; food advertisement and labeling; food testing; food safety risk analysis: prevention, stopping and remedying of food safety incidents; food safety information, education and communication; and responsibilities for state management of food safety.

Interpretation Of Terms

In Law on food safety, the terms below are construed as follows:

1. Food safety means the assurance that food does not cause harm to human health and life.

2. Food-borne disease means a disease caused by eating or drinking a food contaminated with pathogens.

3. Food processing aid means a substance which is intentionally used in the processing of food materials or food ingredients in order to achieve a technological purpose and can be removed from or remains in foods.

4. Food processing means a process of preparing preliminarily processed food or fresh and raw food by an industrial or manual method to create food materials or food products.

5. Catering service establishment means a food-preparing facility, such as shop or stall trading in ready-to-eat food and cooked food restaurant, facility preparing ready-to-eat food portions, canteen or collective kitchen.

6. Conditions for food safety assurance means technical regulations and other regulations applicable to food, food producers and traders and food production and trading activities promulgated by competent state agencies for the purpose of assuring food safety for human health and life.

7. Food testing means the conduct of one or several tests and assessments of the conformity with relevant technical regulations and standards of food, food additives, food processing aids, food fortifiers, packages, tools and food containers.

8. Food trading means the conduct of one, several or all activities of food display, preservation service, transportation service or trading.

8. Food product lot means a specified quantity of a type of products bearing the same name, of the same quality, ingredients and shelf life, and produced by the same producer.

10. Food poisoning means a pathological state caused by absorbing contaminated or poisonous food.

11. Food contamination risk means the possibility that contaminants infiltrate into a food in the course of production or trading.

12. Food contamination means the presence of contaminants in food which are harmful to human health or life.

13. Food additive means a substance with or without nutritious value, which is intentionally added to food in the process of production in order to retain or improve particular characteristics of food.

14. Food production means the conduct of one. several or all activities of cultivation rearing, harvest, fishing, exploitation, preliminary processing, processing, packaging and preservation in order to make food.

15. Primary production means the conduct of one, several or all activities of cultivation, rearing, harvest, fishing and exploitation.

16. Preliminary processing of food means the treatment of cultivated, reared, collected, harvested, fished or exploited products in order to make ready-to-eat fresh and raw food or a food material or semi-finished products for the food processing stage.

17. Food safety incident means a circumstance occurring due to food poisoning, a food-borne disease or another food-induced circumstance which is directly harmful to human health or life.

18. Contaminant means an element which is unwanted and unintentionally added to food and likely to adversely affect food safety.

19. Shelf life means the period before the end of which a food still retains its nutritious value and remains safe under the preservation conditions indicated on its label under the producer's guidance.

20. Food means a product eaten or drunk by humans in fresh and raw, preliminarily processed, processed or preserved form. Food excludes cosmetics, cigarettes and substances used as pharmaceuticals.

21. Fresh and raw food means unprocessed food, including fresh meat, eggs, fish, aquatic products, vegetables, tubers and fruits and other unprocessed foods.

22. Micronutrient-fortified food means food supplemented with vitamins, minerals and trace elements in order to prevent or remedy the harm caused by the deficiency of these substances or elements to the health of the community or a particular group in the community.

23. Functional food means a food used to support a function of the human body, relax the body, boost the immunity against diseases, including supplements, health protection food and medical nutritious food.

24. Genetically modified food means a food containing one or several ingredients which have been genetically engineered.

25. Irradiated food means a food which has been irradiated by a radioactive source to treat the food, preventing it from degeneration.

26. Street food means a food processed for instant consumption and sold by vendors on streets or in public or similar places.

27. Prepackaged food means a food completely packaged and labeled, ready for sale for further processing or instant consumption.

28. Tracing of food origin means the tracking down of the creation and circulation of food.

Principles Of Food Safety Management

1. To assure food safety is the responsibility of all food producers and traders.

2. Food production and trading are conditional activities; and food producers and traders shall bear responsibility for the safety of food they produce or trade in.

3. Food safety management must be based on relevant technical regulations and regulations promulgated by competent state management agencies and applicable standards announced by producers.

4. Food safety management must be conducted throughout the course of food production and trading on the basis of food safety risk analysis.

5. Food safety management must ensure a clear division of responsibilities and powers and inter-sector coordination.

6. Food safety management must meet requirements of socio-economic development.

State Policies On Food Safety

1. To elaborate strategies and master plans on food safety assurance, regarding the planning of zones for safe food production according to the food supply chain as a priority key task.

2. To use state resources and other resources to invest in scientific research and technological application to serve food safety risk analysis; to build new laboratories and upgrade some existing ones up to regional or international standards; to raise the capacity of existing analysis laboratories; to support investment in building zones producing safe food materials, wholesale markets for farm produce and food, and industrial-scale cattle and poultry slaughterhouses.

3. To encourage food producers and traders to renew technologies and expand their production: to produce high-quality and safe food; to fortify food with essential micronutrients: to build their brands and develop their safe food supply systems.

4. To establish a legal framework and realize a roadmap for compulsory application of good manufacturing practices (GMP), good agricultural practices (GAP), good hygiene practices (GHP) and hazard analysis and critical control points (HACCP) and other advanced food safety management systems in food production and trading.

5. To undertake international cooperation, step up the conclusion of treaties and international agreements on accreditation and mutual recognition in the field of food.

6. To promptly commend and reward organizations and individuals that produce or trade in safe foods.

7. To encourage and create conditions for domestic societies, associations, organizations and individuals and foreign organizations and individuals to invest or participate in the elaboration of standards, technical regulations and testing of food safety.

8. To increase investment in and diversify forms and methods of public information and education to raise public awareness about the consumption of safe food, sense of responsibility and business ethics of food producers and traders towards the community.

Prohibited Acts

1. Using for food processing purposes materials other than those permitted for use in food.

2. Using food materials which have passed their shelf life, arc of unclear origin or unsafe for food production and processing.

3. Using food additives or food processing aids which have passed their shelf life or are outside the list of those permitted for use or using permitted additives or food processing aids in excess of allowable dosages: using chemicals of unclear origins or banned chemicals in food production or trading.

4. Using animals which died of diseases, epidemics or unidentified causes or animal carcasses subject to destruction for food production or trading.

5. Producing or trading in:

a/ Food breaching regulations on goods labeling;

b/ Food unconformable with relevant technical regulations:

c/ Degenerated food;

d/ Food containing toxic or hazardous substances or contaminated with toxins or contaminants in excess of allowable limits;

e/ Food which is contaminated for the reason that their packages or containers are unsafe, broken, torn or deformed in the course of transportation;

f/ Meat or meat products which have not yet gone through veterinary inspection or have gone through veterinary inspection but fail to meet requirements;

g/ Food banned from production or trading for the purpose of epidemic prevention and combat;

h/ Food for which regulation conformity declarations have not yet been registered with competent state agencies in case such food subject to regulation conformity declaration registration;

i/ Food which is of unclear origin or has passed its shelf life.

6. Using vehicles which can cause food contamination or vehicles which have transported toxic or hazardous substances but not yet been cleaned up for transporting food materials or foods.

7. Supplying untruthful or forging food testing results.

8. Covering up. falsifying or obliterating scenes or evidence of food safety incidents or committing other acts of intentionally obstructing the detection and remedy of food safety incidents.

9. Employing persons infected with contagious diseases in food production or trading.

10. Producing or trading in food at establishments without certificates of satisfaction of food safety conditions prescribed by law.

11. Advertising food untruthfully or confusingly to consumers.

12. Publishing or publicly notifying misleading information on food safety, thus causing public disparagement or damage to food production and trading.

13. Using illegally roadbeds, pavements. corridors or common yards, passageways and auxiliary spaces for street food processing, producing or trading.

Handling Of Violations Of The Law On Food Safety

Food producers and traders that violate the law on food safely shall, depending on the nature and severity of their violations, be administratively handled or examined for penal liability. If causing damage, they shall pay compensations and remedy consequences under law.

Rights And Obligations Of Food Producers

1. Food producers have the following rights:

a/ To decide on and announce standards of products they produce and supply; to decide on application of internal control measures to assure food safety;

b/ To request food traders to cooperate in recalling and disposing of unsafe food;

c/ To select conformity assessment organizations and testing establishments already designated to certify regulation conformity;

d/ To use standard conformity stamps and regulation conformity stamps and other marks for their products under law;

e/ To lodge complaints and denunciations and file lawsuits under law;

f/ To get compensations for damage under law.

2. Food producers have the following obligations:

a/ To comply with conditions for food safety assurance, assure food safety in the process of production, and take responsibility for the safety of food they produce;

b/ To comply with the Government's regulations on fortification of micronutrients the deficiency of which will affect community health;

c/ To provide adequate and accurate information on products on their labels and packages or in documents accompanying food under the law on goods labeling;

d/ To establish a self-inspection process in the course of food production:

e/ To provide truthful information on food safety: to give timely, adequate and accurate warnings about the risk of food to become unsafe and provide preventive methods for sellers and consumers; to notify requirements on the transportation, storage, preservation and use of food:

f/ To promptly suspend food production, notify concerned parties of and take consequence remedies upon detecting unsafe food or food unconformable with announced standards or relevant technical regulations:

g/ To keep dossiers, food samples and necessary information under regulations on tracing of food origin; to comply with regulations on tracing of origins of unsafe foods;

h/ To recall and dispose of food which has passed their shelf life or are unsafe. In case foods are to be destroyed, the food destruction must comply with the law on environmental protection and other relevant laws and food producers shall bear all expenses for destruction;

i/ To comply with law as well as. inspection or examination decisions of competent state agencies;

j/ To pay sampling and testing expenses as prescribed in Article 48 of Law on food safety;

k/ To pay compensations under law for damage caused by unsafe food they produce.

Rights And Obligations Of Food Traders

1. Foods traders have the following rights:

a/ To decide on internal control measures to maintain food quality, hygiene and safety;

b/ To request food producers and importers to cooperate in recalling and disposing of unsafe food:

c/ To select testing establishments to inspect food safety; to select testing establishments already designated for certification of regulation conformity for imported food;

d/ To lodge complaints and denunciations and file lawsuits under law;

e/ To get compensations for damage under law.

2. Foods traders have the following obligations:

a/ To comply with conditions for food safety assurance in the course of trading and take responsibility for the safety of food they trade in;

b/ To inspect food origins and labels and documents related to food safety; to keep dossiers on food; to comply with regulations on tracing of origins of unsafe food;

c/ To supply truthful information of food safety; to notify consumers of safety assurance conditions in the course of food transportation, storage, preservation and use:

d/ To promptly provide information on risks of food to become unsafe and methods of risk prevention to consumers upon receiving warnings of food producers or importers;

e/ To promptly suspend their trading operation and inform food producers or importers and consumers of unsafe food upon detecting such food:

f/ To promptly report to a competent agency on a food poisoning or a disease borne by foods they trade in and promptly remedy its consequences upon detecting it;

g/ To cooperate with food producers and importers and competent state agencies in investigating food poisoning cases in order to remedy consequences, recall or dispose of unsafe food;

h/ To comply with law as well as inspection or examination decisions of competent state agencies;

i/ To pay food sampling and testing expenses;

j/ To pay compensations under law for damage caused by unsafe food they trade in.

Rights And Obligations Of Food Consumers

1. Food consumers have the following rights:

a/ To be provided with truthful information on food safety, and appropriate instructions for food use. transportation, storage, preservation, selection and use; to be informed of risks of food to become unsafe and methods of risk prevention upon receiving warnings;

b/ To request food producers and traders to protect their interests under law;

c/ To request consumer interest protection organizations to protect their lawful rights and interests under the law on consumer interest protection:

d/To lodge complaints and denunciations and file lawsuits under law;

e/ To get compensations under law for their damage caused by consumption of unsafe food.

2. Food consumers have the following obligations:

a/ To fully comply with regulations and guidance of food producers and traders on food safety in transportation, storage, preservation and use:

b/ To promptly provide information on risks of food to become unsafe upon detecting these risks, and report food poisonings and food-home diseases to the nearest medical examination and treatment establishments, competent state agencies and food producers and traders:

c/ To comply with the law on environmental protection in the course of food consumption.

General Conditions On Food Safety Assurance

1. To conform with relevant technical regulations, to meet limit requirements for pathogenic microorganisms, residues of plant protection drugs or veterinary drugs, heavy metals, contaminants and other substances in food that may cause harm to human health and life.

2. Depending on each type of food, food must comply with one or more of the following regulations:

a/ Regulations on use of food additives and processing aids in food production and trading:

b/ Regulations on food packaging and labeling;

c/ Regulations on food preservation.

Safety Assurance Conditions For Fresh And Raw Food

To have veterinary hygiene certificates issued by competent veterinary agencies for fresh and raw food of animal origin under the animal health law.

Safety Assurance Conditions For Processed Food

1. Original materials of food must be safe and retain their inherent properties. Materials forming a food must not interact with one another to create products harmful to human health and life.

2. Prepackaged processed food must have regulation conformity announcements registered with competent state agencies prior to market sale.

The Government shall specify the registration of regulation conformity announcements of prepackaged processed food and their validity term.

Safety Assurance Conditions For Micronutrient-Fortified Food

1. Original materials of food must be safe and retain their inherent properties. Materials forming a food must not interact with one another to create products harmful to human health and life.

2. Only micronutrients being vitamins, minerals and trace elements may be added to food with a content unharmful to human health and life.

Safety Assurance Conditions For Functional Foods

1. To have scientific information and documents proving the effects of their ingredients that create the announced functions.

2. Functional foods which are first put on market sale must have a report on testing of their effect.

3. The Minister of Health shall specify the management of functional foods.

Safety Assurance Conditions For Food Additives And Processing Aids

1. To conform with relevant technical regulations, to comply with regulations on food additives and processing aids.

2. To have use instructions written on their labels or inserts in each product unit in any language depending on the origin of products.

3. To be on the list of food additives and processing aids permitted for use in food production and trading.

4. To register regulation conformity announcements with competent state agencies prior to market sale.

The Government shall specify the registration of regulation conformity announcements and their validity term for food additives and processing aids.

Safety Assurance Conditions For Food-Packaging Tools And Food Packages And Containers

1. To be made of safe materials, guaranteeing that they do not release toxic substances, strange smell or taste into food, and they preserve food quality within the shelf life.

2. To conform with relevant technical regulations, to meet the regulations on food-packaging tools and food packages and containers.

3. To register regulation conformity announcements with competent state agencies prior to market sale.

The Government shall specify the registration of regulation conformity announcements and their validity term for food-packaging tools and food packages and containers.

Food Safety Assurance Conditions For Food Producers And Traders

Food producers and traders must meet the following conditions:

a/ Having suitable venues with appropriate areas and safety distance from toxic and contaminating sources and other harmful factors;

b/ Having sufficient technically qualified water for food production and trading:

c/ Having adequate appropriate equipment to process materials and process, package, preserve and transport different types of food: having adequate washing and sterilization equipment and tools, disinfecting fluid, and equipment for preventing and controlling insects and harmful animals;

d/ Having a waste treatment system which operates regularly under the law on environmental protection:

e/ Maintaining food safety assurance conditions and keeping records of source and origin of food materials and other documents on the entire food production and trading process;

f/ Complying with regulations on health, knowledge and practices of persons directly engaged in food production and trading.

Food Safety Assurance Conditions For Food Preservation

Food producers and traders must meet the following conditions for food preservation:

a/ Having preservation places and means which are large enough to preserve each type of food separately, allow technically safe and precise loading and unloading and guarantee preservation hygiene:

b/ Preventing the effects of temperature, humidity, insects, animals, dust, strange smell and negative environmental effects: guaranteeing sufficient light: having special-use equipment for adjusting temperature, humidity and other climate conditions, ventilation equipment and other special preservation conditions required by each type of food;

c/ Complying with preservation regulations of food producers and traders.

Food Safety Assurance Conditions For Food Transportation

1. Organizations and individuals transporting food must meet the following conditions:

a/ Means for transporting foods are made of materials which do not contaminate food and food packages and are easy to clean;

b/ Food preservation conditions as required by food producers and traders are maintained throughout the course of transportation;

c/ Food is not transported together with toxic goods or goods which may cause cross-contamination and affect food quality.

2. Competent state management agencies shall provide means for transporting food and routes for transporting fresh and raw food in urban areas.

Food Safety Assurance Conditions For Small-Scale Food Production And Trading

Small-scale food producers and traders must meet the following food safety assurance conditions:

a/ Ensuring safely distance from toxic and contaminating sources:

b/ Having sufficient technically qualified water for food production and trading:

c/ Having appropriate equipment for food production and trading which neither harm nor contaminate food;

d/ Using materials, chemicals, food additives, processing aids, food-packaging tools and food packages and containers in preliminary processing, processing and preservation of food;

e/ Complying with regulations on health, knowledge and practices of persons directly engaged in food production and trading:

f/ Collecting and treating waste under the law on environmental protection;

g/ Maintaining food safety assurance conditions and storing trading-related information to ensure the tracing of food origin.

Food Safety Assurance Conditions For Producers Of Fresh And Raw Food

Producers of fresh and raw food must meet the following conditions:

a/ Meeting requirements on cultivation land, water sources and production places for producing safe food;

b/ Complying with the laws on use of plant varieties and livestock breeds; fertilizer, animal feed, plant protection drugs, veterinary drugs, growth, weight and sexual maturity stimulants, food preservatives and other food safety-related substances;

c/ Complying with regulations on animal quarantine and hygiene in animal slaughtering; and plant quarantine for crop products;

d/ Treating waste under the law on environmental protection:

e/ Using detergents, disinfectants and antidotes which are safe for humans and the environment;

f/ Maintaining food safety assurance conditions, keeping records of source and origin of food materials and other documents on the entire process to produce fresh and raw food.

Food Safety Assurance Conditions For Traders Of Fresh And Raw Food

Traders of fresh and raw food must meet the following conditions:

a/ Meeting safety assurance conditions for food-packaging tools and food packages and containers and for food preservation and transportation specified in the Law on food safety;

b/ Ensuring and maintaining hygiene in business places.

Food Safety Assurance Conditions For Traders Of Processed Food

1. Traders of prepackaged processed food must meet the following conditions:

a/ Complying with regulations on food labeling:

b/ Meeting the safety assurance conditions for food-packaging tools and food packages and containers and for food preservation;

c/ Ensuring and maintaining hygiene in business places;

d/ Preserving food as required by producers.

2. Traders of non-prepackaged processed food must meet the following conditions:

a/ Adopting measures to ensure that food is neither spoiled, moldy nor in contact with insects, animals, dust and other contaminants;

b/ Washing or sterilizing the tableware and food containers before use of instant food;

c/ Obtaining information on the origin and production date of food.

Food Safety Assurance Conditions For Food Processing Places And Commercial Provision Of Catering Services

1. Kitchens are arranged in a way to ensure that unprocessed and processed food is not cross-contaminated.

2. Having sufficient technically qualified water for food processing and trading.

3. Having hygienic devices for collecting and containing garbage and waste.

4. Sewers in the areas of shops and kitchens must be drained without any stagnancy.

5. Eating rooms must be airy. cool, sufficiently lit and kept clean and have equipment to prevent insects and harmful animals.

6. Having food preservation equipment and toilets and collecting waste and garbage daily.

7. Heads of units having collective kitchens shall take responsibility for food safety.

Food Safety Assurance Conditions For Food Processors And Catering Services Providers

1. To have separate utensils and containers for raw and cooked food.

2. To ensure safety and hygiene of cooking and processing utensils.

3. The tableware must be made of safe materials and kept clean and dry.

4. To comply with regulations on health, knowledge and practices of persons directly engaged in food production and trading.

Food Safety Assurance Conditions For Food Processing And Preservation

1. To use safe food and food materials of clear origin and keep food samples.

2. To process food safely and hygienically.

3. Food on sale must be placed in glass showcases or hygienic preservation containers on tables or shelves above the ground, which can prevent dust, rain, sunshine, insects and harmful animals.

Food Safety Assurance Conditions For Street Food Display Places

1. To be separated from toxic and contaminating sources.

2. To display food on tables, shelves or means which meet requirements on food hygiene and safety and street landscape.

Food Safety Assurance Conditions For Food Materials And Containers, Eating Utensils, Food Containers And Street Vendors

1. Materials for processing street food must meet food safety requirements and have clear source and origin.

2. Eating utensils and food containers must be hygienically safe.

3. Packages and materials in direct contact with food must neither contaminate nor release contaminants into food.

4. To have devices to prevent sunshine, rain, dust, insects and harmful animals.

5. To sufficiently have technically qualified water for food processing and trading.

6. To comply with regulations on health, knowledge and practices of persons directly engaged in food production and trading.

Establishments And Conditions For The Grant And Withdrawal Of Certificates Of Food Safety Eligibility

1. An establishment shall be granted a certificate of food safety eligibility when it fully meets the following conditions:

a/ Having adequate conditions for assuring food safety suitable to each type of food production and trading;

b/ Having registered for food production and trading as indicated in its business registration certificate.

2. An organization or individual shall have its/his/her certificate of food safety eligibility withdrawn when it/he/she no longer satisfies all conditions prescribed by law.

3. The Government shall specify establishments not subject to the grant of certificates of food safety eligibility.

Order, Procedures And Methods Of State Inspection Of Food Safety With Regard To Imported Food

1. The order of and procedures for state inspection of food safety with regard to imported food, food additives, processing aids, food-packaging tools, food packages and containers comply with the law on product and goods quality and the following provisions:

a/ Food may be transported to warehouses for preservation pending customs clearance only when they have a registration for food safety inspection:

b/ Customs clearance shall only be effected when there is a written certification of satisfaction of import requirements.

2. Modes of state inspection of food safety for imported food, food additives, processing aids, food-packaging tools, food packages and containers:

a/ Tightened inspection:

b/ Normal inspection;

c/ Reduced inspection.

Food Advertisement

1. Food advertisement shall be carried out by food producers and traders or advertisement service providers under the law on advertisement.

2. Before registering for food advertisement, organizations and individuals that have food to be advertised shall send dossiers to competent state management agencies for certification of advertisement contents.

3. Advertisement makers, advertisement service providers and organizations and individuals with to-be-advertised food may only make advertisement after the advertisement contents are appraised, and must strictly comply with certified contents.

Expenses For Food Sampling And Testing

1. Expenses for food sampling and testing to serve food safety examination and inspection shall be paid by agencies that decide on such examination and inspection.

2. Based on testing results, if agencies that decide on food safety examination and inspection conclude that food producers or traders violate the law on food safety, the violators shall refund food sampling and testing expenses to the examination and inspection agencies.

3. Organizations and individuals that request food sampling and testing shall themselves pay expenses for food sampling and testing.

4. Expenses for food sampling and testing in food safety-related disputes or complaints shall be paid by petitioners or complainants. When testing results affirm that food producers or traders violate regulations on food safety, the violators shall refund expenses for sampling and testing of foods involved in disputes to the petitioners or complainants.

Objects Subject To Analysis Of Food Safety Risks

1. Foods of high poisoning rate.

2. Foods with samples taken for surveillance showing high rate of violating technical regulations on food safety.

3. Food production or trading environment or establishments which are suspected of causing pollution.

4. Foods or food production or trading establishments which are subject to risk analysis to meet management requirements.

Analysis Of Food Safety Risks

1. Analysis of food safety risks covers assessment, management and communication of risks to food safety.

2. Assessment of food safety risks covers:

a/ Investigating and testing to identify hazards to food safety which belong to groups of microbiological, chemical and physical agents;

b/ Identifying risks of health hazards to food safety, extent and scope of impacts of hazards on the community health.

3. Management of food safety risks covers:

a/ Implementing solutions to limiting food safety risks in each stage of the food supply chain;

b/ Controlling and coordinating to limit food safety risks in providing catering services and conducting other food production or trading activities.

4. Communication on food safety risks covers:

a/ Providing information on preventive measures in cases of food poisoning or unsafe food-borne diseases to raise public awareness about and responsibility for food safety risks;

b/ Notifying or forecasting food safety risks; building an information system for warning food safety risks and food-borne diseases.

Prevention Of Food Safety Incidents

1. Organizations and individuals that detect signs of a food safety incident shall immediately notify it to the nearest health establishment or a competent state agency for taking prompt preventive measures.

2. Measures to prevent food safety incidents include:

a/ Ensuring safety in the process of food production, trading and consumption;

b/ Educating, propagating and disseminating food safety-related knowledge and practices to producers, traders and consumers;

c/ Examining and inspecting food safety in food production and trading;

d/ Analyzing food contamination risks;

e/ Investigating, surveying and storing data on food safety:

f/ Storing food samples.

Remedy Of Food Safety Incidents

1. Organizations and individuals that detect a food safety incident occurring at home or overseas shall declare it to the nearest health establishment for taking prompt remedies.

2. Remedies for food safety incidents include:

a/ Promptly detecting, and giving first aid and medical treatment to. poisoned persons or persons infected with food-borne diseases or in other food-induced circumstances harmful to human health or life:

b/ Investigating cases of food poisoning, identifying causes of poisoning and food-borne diseases and tracing the origin of poisoning or disease-transmitting food;

c/ Suspending production or trading activities:

recalling and disposing of poisoning or disease-transmitting food being marketed;

d/ Notifying food poisoning and food-borne diseases to concerned organizations and individuals:

e/ Taking measures to prevent risks of food poisoning and food-borne diseases.

3. Suppliers of poisoning foods shall pay all medical treatment expenses for poisoned persons and pay compensations under the civil law.

Tracing Of The Origin Of Unsafe Foods

1. Food producers and traders shall trace the origin of unsafe foods in the following cases:

a/ At the request of competent state agencies;

b/ When detecting that food products they produce or trade in are unsafe.

2. Food producers and traders that trace the origin of unsafe foods shall:

a/ Identify and notify lots of unsafe food products:

b/ Request food trading agents to report on the quantity of products of unsafe food lots, actual quantities of products left in stock and being marketed:

c/ Summarize, and report to competent state agencies on. recall plans and disposal measures.

3. Competent state agencies shall inspect and supervise the tracing of the origin of unsafe foods.

Recall And Disposal Of Unsafe Foods

1. The following foods shall be recalled:

a/ Foods which are still marketed after their shelf life:

b/ Foods unconformable with relevant technical regulations;

c/ Foods being new technological products not yet been permitted for circulation;

d/ Foods which are degenerated during preservation, transportation or trading;

e/ Foods which contain substances banned from use or in which appear contaminants in excess of allowable limits;

f/ Imported foods which are notified by a competent authority of the exporting country or another country or an international organization to contain contaminants harmful to human health and life.

2. Recall of unsafe foods takes the following forms:

a/ Voluntary recall by food producers or traders themselves:

b/ Compulsory recall by food producers and traders at the request of competent state agencies.

3. Unsafe foods shall be disposed of through:

a/ Correction of product flaws or labeling errors:

b/ Change of use purposes;

c/ Re-export:

d/ Destruction.

4. Unsafe food producers and traders shall publish information on recalled products, recall and dispose of unsafe foods within the time limit decided by a competent state agency, and pay all recall and disposal expenses.

Past the prescribed time limit, food producers and traders that fail to recall foods shall be coerced to do so under law.

5. Competent state agencies shall:

a/ Based on the severity of violations of safety assurance conditions, decide on the recall and disposal of unsafe foods as well as the time limit for completing such recall and disposal;

b/ Inspect the recall of unsafe foods:

c/ Handle violations of the law on food safety according to their competence as defined by law:

d/ For food products which are likely to seriously affect the community health or in other emergency cases, directly recall and dispose of them and request their producers and traders to pay recall and disposal expenses.

Purposes And Requirements Of Information, Education And Communication On Food Safety

1. Information, education and communication on food safety aims to raise public awareness about food safety, and change backward behaviors, customs and practices in production, trading and living which cause food unsafely, contributing to protecting human health and life; and about business ethics and responsibility of food producers and traders towards consumer health and life.

2. Information, education and communication on food safety must be:

a/ Accurate, prompt, explicit, simple and practical;

b/ Suitable to the nation's traditions, culture and identity, religions, social ethics, beliefs, customs and practices;

c/ Suitable to each category of targeted subjects.

Contents Of Information, Education And Communication On Food Safety

1. Providing, propagating and disseminating knowledge and law on food safety.

2. Providing information on causes and ways of identifying food poisoning risks, food-borne diseases and measures to prevent and remedy food safety incidents.

3. Providing information on exemplary models of safe food production or trading; recall of unsafe foods, and handling of establishments that seriously violate the law on food safety.

Entities Eligible To Access Information, Education And Communication On Food Safety

1. All organizations and individuals have the right to access information, education and communication on food safety.

2. Priority will be given to the following entities in accessing information, education and communication on food safety:

a/ Food consumers;

b/ Managers and executive officers of food production or trading establishments; food producers and traders;

c/ Fresh and raw food producers and traders and small-scale food producers and traders;

Forms Of Information, Education And Communication On Food Safety

1. Through competent state agencies in charge of food safety.

2. In the mass media.

3. Integration in teaching and learning activities at educational institutions of the national education system.

4. Through cultural and community activities and activities of mass organizations and social organizations, and other forms of public cultural activities.

5. Through food safety-related inquiry points at line ministries.

Food Safety Inspection

1. Food safety inspection is specialized inspection. Food safety inspection shall be conducted by the health; agriculture and rural development; and industry and trade sectors under the law on inspection.

2. The Government shall specify the coordination among food safety inspectorates of ministries and ministerial-level agencies with other forces in ensuring food safety.

Contents Of Food Safety Inspection

1. Compliance with technical standards and regulations on food safety applicable to food production and trading and food products promulgated by competent state agencies.

2. Compliance with relevant food safety standards announced by food producers for application to food production and trading and food products.

3. Advertising and labeling of food within the scope of management.

4. Regulation conformity certification and food safety testing.

5. Compliance with other legal provisions on food safety.

Food Safety Examination

Food safety examination must ensure the following principles:

a/ Objectivity, accuracy, publicity, transparency and non-discrimination.

b/ Keeping confidential information, documents and results of examination related to inspected agencies and food producers and traders pending the availability of official conclusions;

c/ Causing no troubles to food producers and traders.

d/ Taking responsibility before law for relevant examination results and conclusions.

Conclusion

Thank you again for downloading this book on *"LAW ON FOOD SAFETY: Essential Legal Terms Explained You Need To Know About Law On Food Safety!"* and reading all the way to the end. I'm extremely grateful.

If you know of anyone else who may benefit from the informative legal words presented in this book, please help me inform them of this book. I would greatly appreciate it.

Finally, if you enjoyed this book and feel that it has added value to your study or career in any way, please take a couple of minutes to share your thoughts and post a REVIEW on Amazon. Your feedback will help me to continue to write the kind of Kindle books that helps you get results. Furthermore, if you write a simple REVIEW with positive words for this book on Amazon, you can help hundreds or perhaps thousands of other readers who may want to enhance their legal vocabulary have a chance getting what they need. Like you, they worked hard for every penny they spend on books. With the information and recommendation you provide, they would be more likely to take action right away. We really look forward to reading your review.

Thanks again for your support and good luck!

If you enjoy my book, please write a POSITIVE REVIEW on amazon.

-- Dr. Peter Johnson --

Check Out Other Books

Go here to check out other related books that might interest you:

**Legal Terminology And Phrases: Essential Legal Terms Explained
You Need To Know About Crimes, Penalty And Criminal Procedure**

http://www.amazon.com/dp/B01L5EB54Y

LAW ON INTELLECTUAL PROPERTY: Essential Legal Terms
Explained You Need To Know About Trademarks, Copyrights,
Patents, and Trade Secrets!

https://www.amazon.com/dp/B07PFP3MDY

COMPANY LAW: Mastering Essential Legal Terms Explained About Limited Liability Companies, Joint-Stock Companies, Partnership, Private Enterprises, And Groups of Companies!

https://www.amazon.com/dp/B07P2PRVMJ

TAX LAW: Essential Legal Terms Explained You Need To Know About Types of Tax Law!

https://www.amazon.com/dp/B07PH1L3RS

INVESTMENT LAW: Essential Legal Terms Explained You Need
To Know About Law On Investment!

https://www.amazon.com/dp/B07P79D925

LABOR LAW: Essential Legal Terms Explained You Need To Know
About Law On Labor!

https://www.amazon.com/dp/B07PFD2CML

CIVIL LAW: Mastering Essential Legal Terms Explained About
Civil Rights, Guardianship, Civil Transactions, Civil Obligations,
Civil Liability, Civil Contracts And Civil Procedure!

https://www.amazon.com/dp/B07P5GS8LD

LAW ON LAWYERS : Essential Legal Terms Explained You Need To Know About Law on Lawyers!

https://www.amazon.com/dp/B07PH9SCBN

CHILDREN LAW: Essential Legal Terms Explained You Need To Know About Law on Children!

https://www.amazon.com/dp/B07Q4T26R5

Legal Vocabulary In Use: Master 600+ Essential Legal Terms And Phrases Explained In 10 Minutes A Day

http://www.amazon.com/dp/B01L0FKXPU

Civil Law Vocabulary In Use: Master 350+ Essential Civil Law Terms
And Phrases Explained With Examples In 10 Minutes A Day.

https://www.amazon.com/dp/B0781TQWGV

Criminal Law Vocabulary In Use: Master 400+ Essential Criminal

Law Terms And Phrases Explained With Examples In 10 Minutes A

Day.

https://www.amazon.com/dp/B078KLR51Z

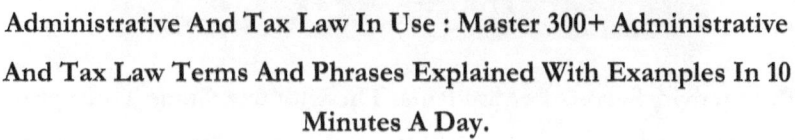

Administrative And Tax Law In Use : Master 300+ Administrative
And Tax Law Terms And Phrases Explained With Examples In 10
Minutes A Day.

https://www.amazon.com/dp/B07JMD546J

Productivity Secrets For Students: The Ultimate Guide To Improve
Your Mental Concentration, Kill Procrastination, Boost Memory And
Maximize Productivity In Study

http://www.amazon.com/dp/B01JS52UT6

Shortcut To Ielts Writing: The Ultimate Guide To Immediately Increase Your Ielts Writing Scores

http://www.amazon.com/dp/B01JV7EQGG

www.ingramcontent.com/pod-product-compliance
Lightning Source LLC
Chambersburg PA
CBHW030728180526
45157CB00008BA/3096